Library of Congress Catalogue Number: 2017902475

ISBN: 978-0-9987371-0-2

Pandergy Publishing LLC
9722 Groffs Mill Drive
Unit #513
Owings Mills, MD 21117
(443) 261-5410
pandergypublishingllc@gmail.com
http://pandergypublishingllc.com

Printed in the United States of America.
1 3 5 7 9 10 8 6 4 2

Dedicated to those who love
to let loose and have a ball.

Come learn a few facts about dear Uncle Jack.
Attached to his stick sits a big hairy sack.

The banana he carries
is unusually long.

His right hand is weak,
but his left hand is strong.

Oh, my Uncle Jack has many interesting quirks,
like the way his eye winks when his hand starts to jerk
as he's waving his arm back and forth with a cry
towards all of the people who go passing by.

Come along with my uncle up over the hills
to learn all about how he gets all of his thrills!

We'll spend the whole day seeing where he will roam.
Let's start off by going to Uncle Jack's home!

It's as bald as an eagle.
It stands tall and acts regal,
though its wrinkles and veins look absurd.

My Uncle Jack's off in his shiny new car.
There's the movies, the woods, and behind a snack bar,
leaving a white sticky trail down below.
Let's follow it closely
and see where he goes!

My Uncle Jack's off in the grocery store.
He leaves a big puddle all over the floor.
From his clothes to his boots he is wet from the rain.
He's making a mess!
Oh, what a pain!!

Grabbing at nuts with a whimsical smile,
shooting whipped cream as he runs down the aisle,

and just as he heads out the door...
He sees two old ladies named Helen and Ellen
and watches them squeeze their plump, juicy ripe melons...

Then my Uncle Jack's off once more!

My Uncle Jack loves to play all kinds of sports.
He puts on a pair of loose-fitting golf shorts.
He heads to the green with some big lofty goals.
My Uncle Jack wants to get in 18 holes.

Swinging his stick on the golf course, of course,
smacking his balls with a glorious force,
driving them far with a grunt and a yell,
no one can see where they went to or fell.

The time to move on is now close at hand.
He's looking around... where did the shots land?
Oh, there's one on the green! And there's one on the sand!
Now my Uncle Jack's off with two balls in his hand.

Uncle Jack's a fine jockey
who's fast and quite cocky,
his mighty steed gallops 'round the course.

Hooray! He won the big race!
But his foot's stuck in place.
Won't someone please help my Uncle Jack off the horse?

My Uncle Jack loves to have fun and get silly
when he hangs with his two best friends Peter and Willy.
They take off their raincoats made out of lambskin
to play tug of war.
"Grab our rope! Let's begin!"

So many adventures have gone and transpired.
My Uncle Jack's off so much that he's tired.
He yawns and begins counting sheep in his head.
He snuggles in deeply. It's now time for bed!

He starts to imagine
the fuzzy white creatures,
and how he would pet
their soft delicate features,
He strokes each one gently,
they bleat and they peep.
With a Boom! and a Bang!

My Uncle Jack's off to sleep.

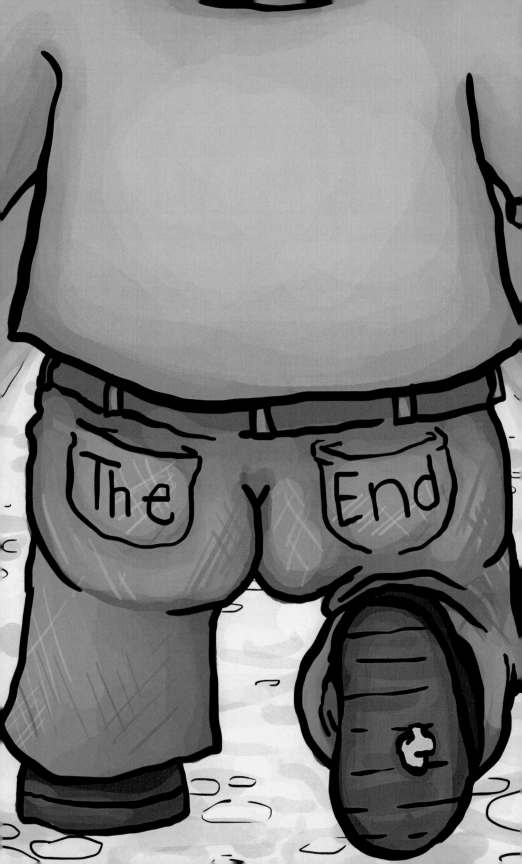